SHANNON HALE

REAL FRIENDS

Artwork by
LeUYEN PHAM

Color by **JANE POOLE**

:01

First Second
New York

P9-CSW-584

LIBRARY OF CONGRESS CONTROL NUMBER: 2016945552

PAPERBACK ISBN: 978-1-62672-785-4
HARDCOVER ISBN: 978-1-62672-416-7

OUR BOOKS MAY BE PURCHASED IN BULK FOR PROMOTIONAL, EDUCATIONAL, OR BUSINESS USE.
PLEASE CONTACT YOUR LOCAL BOOKSELLER OR THE MACMILLAN CORPORATE AND PREMIUM SALES DEPARTMENT
AT (800) 221-7945 EXT. 5442 OR BY E-MAIL AT MACMILLANSPECIALMARKETS@MACMILLAN.COM.

FIRST EDITION 2017
BOOK DESIGN BY LEUYEN PHAM AND ANDREW ARNOLD
COLOR BY JANE POOLE

PRINTED IN CHINA BY TOPPAN LEEFUNG PRINTING LTD.,
DONGGUAN CITY, GUANGDONG PROVINCE

INKED WITH BLACK INDIA INK AND HUNT 103 NIB ON
BRISTOL PAPER AND COLORED DIGITALLY IN ADOBE PHOTOSHOP

PAPERBACK: 10
HARDCOVER: 10   9   8   7   6   5

FOR YOU
WHEN YOU'RE FEELING LONELY AND WORRIED
SO YOU'LL REMEMBER THAT YOU'RE NOT ALONE
—S. H.

FOR SHANNON
—L. P.

ADRIENNE

4

MOM USED TO TELL PEOPLE THAT I WAS "SHY." BUT SUDDENLY, I WASN'T ANYMORE.

I HAD A FRIEND.

ADRIENNE!

AND SHE WAS ALL MINE.

LEAVE HER ALONE, YOU BIG MEANY!

WE HAD THE BEST ADVENTURES TOGETHER.

LET'S GO DOWNSTAIRS.

OKAY.

WE CAN PRETEND WE'RE DALLAS COWBOY CHEERLEADERS.

I DIDN'T UNDERSTAND WHAT EXACTLY DALLAS COWBOY CHEERLEADERS WERE, BUT ON A TV SHOW I'D SEEN, ALL GIRLS WANTED TO BE ONE.
SO I WANTED TO BE ONE TOO. IF I COULD ALSO BE SUPER STRONG.
PLEASE LOVE US!!!
NO WAY, WE'RE TOO BUSY TO BE LOVEY!

15

ADRIENNE!

I LOVED ADRIENNE SO MUCH.

I JUST WANTED TO KISS HER.

I DIDN'T EVER DO IT AGAIN.

BY SECOND GRADE, I WASN'T THE ONLY ONE WHO WANTED ADRIENNE ALL TO MYSELF.

HOW ABOUT TODAY WE PLAY WONDER WOMAN?

POW!

25

32

LATER I FELT BAD THAT I DIDN'T HUG TAMMY OR ANYTHING.

BUT I WAS WAY TOO EXCITED.

ADRIENNE!

MY WISHES HAD COME TRUE.

ATLAS MOVING

JEN

FIRST DAY OF THIRD GRADE, AND I WAS SO HAPPY...

ADRIENNE WAS BACK!

ONE GOOD FRIEND. MY MOM SAYS THAT'S ALL ANYONE REALLY NEEDS.

BUT I WASN'T HER ONLY FRIEND.

THOUGH MY SCHOOL WAS FULL OF JENNIFERS...

JENNIFER F.

JENNY R.

JENNY B.

JENNIFER B.

JENNIFER S.

JENNI M.

...THERE WAS ONLY ONE JEN.

JEN AND ADRIENNE HAD A LOT IN COMMON.

SMART PRETTY CONFIDENT

I COULD SEE WHY ADRIENNE MIGHT WANT JEN AS A BEST FRIEND INSTEAD OF ME.

JEN DANCED BALLET.

SHE PLAYED FLUTE...

...AND PIANO.

SHE WAS THE FASTEST RUNNER AT RECESS RACES.

GASP!

SHE NEVER SEEMED TO GET HURT OR SAD.

PHEW!

UNLIKE...

WAAAH!

BUT JEN ALREADY HAD A BEST FRIEND: JENNY.

YOU'RE SUCH A BABY, SHANNON.

SO MAYBE JEN WOULDN'T TAKE ADRIENNE AWAY FROM ME.

41

OF COURSE ADRIENNE WAS A MEMBER.

BUT I WASN'T SURE IF I WAS.

COME ON, ADRIENNE!

OKAY!

43

MY FAMILY DIDN'T EXACTLY LINE UP LIKE JEN
HAD HER FRIENDS DO AT SCHOOL...

...BUT I WAS USED TO FEELING IN LAST PLACE.

♪ NO BEARS ARE OUT TONIGHT, DADDY SHOT THEM ALL LAST NIGHT... ♪

SOMETIMES, I EVEN FELT SCARED.

SHANNON, YOU GO THAT WAY, WE'LL GO THIS WAY.

BUT...BUT...

NO BEARS ARE OUT TONIGHT...

...DADDY SHOT THEM...

...ALL... LAST...

THE LINEUP BEGAN TO CHANGE.

1 2 3 4 5 6 7

ANOTHER OF THE GROUP'S UNSPOKEN RULES: NO PLAYING WITH NON-GROUPERS.

I'M GOING TO HEIDI'S HOUSE AFTER SCHOOL TODAY.

HEIDI? OH...

WHAT?

YOU KNOW WHAT YOU'LL BE PLAYING...DOLLIES.

IS PLAYING WITH DOLLS BAD OR SOMETHING?

HEY HEIDI!

I'M EXCITED FOR YOU TO COME OVER!

59

NO MATTER HOW WENDY TREATED ME...

SLAM!

...I WAS DETERMINED TO BE RIGHTEOUS, JUST LIKE THE PROPHETS.

WENDY?

WHAT?

I JUST WANTED TO TELL YOU...

...THAT I FORGIVE YOU.

I DIDN'T GET WHY THAT MADE HER MADDER.

JEN'S BIG BROTHERS AND SISTERS SURE HAD WON A LOT OF FIRST PLACE TROPHIES.

JEN HAD ASKED JENNY AND ADRIENNE FIRST, BUT THEY COULDN'T GO. I GUESS I'D MOVED FORWARD IN THE LINEUP.

JENNY

JUST BEFORE FOURTH GRADE STARTED...

E...P...NO WAIT, F.

OR IS IT H?

I COULD SEE EVERYTHING MORE CLEARLY.

THE LEAVES ON TREES.

THE MOUNTAINS.

MY FRIENDS.

I WAS SO EXCITED FOR THIS SCHOOL YEAR. THE ENTIRE GROUP WAS TOGETHER IN ONE FOURTH-GRADE CLASS! JEN AND I WERE GOOD FRIENDS! AND I COULD SEE!

JENNY AND I HAD A LOT IN COMMON.

WE WERE BOTH SORTA POPULAR BECAUSE OF OUR MORE-POPULAR BEST FRIENDS. THOUGH HER WAY MORE THAN ME.

HAND-ME-DOWNS

HAND-ME-DOWNS

NEW CLOTHES

WE WERE BOTH SQUASHED-IN-THE-MIDDLE CHILDREN. I HAD FOUR SIBLINGS. JENNY HAD EIGHT.

71

I HAD TROUBLE KEEPING TRACK...

...OF WHEN I WAS IN...

...AND WHEN I WAS OUT.

EMILY.

SARAH.

UM...I DON'T NEED ANYONE ELSE ON MY TEAM.

HEY WENDY! CAN
WE HAVE SOME--

85

OR WOULD I BE OUT FOR GOOD?

ALL A PERSON NEEDS IS ONE GOOD FRIEND.

BUT IF I WASN'T IN THE GROUP...

I'D LOSE ADRIENNE.

86

THERE WAS ONE GROUP OF FOURTH GRADE BOYS EQUAL IN POPULARITY TO THE GROUP.

WE WEREN'T EXACTLY FRIENDS WITH THEM.

BECAUSE OF COOTIES, I GUESS. WHATEVER COOTIES WERE.

BUT WE DID CALL THEM. ANONYMOUSLY.

HI, IS GREG THERE?

HI GREG, THIS IS A RATING CALL.

WHAT DO YOU RATE JEN ON LOOKS AND PERSONALITY?

Jen
Looks 10
Personality 10

THE BOYS NEVER RATING-CALLED US. I GUESS THEY DIDN'T CARE WHAT WE THOUGHT ABOUT THEM.

LET'S CALL...

...JUSTIN NOW.

HELLO?

WHAT DO YOU RATE JEN ON LOOKS AND PERSONALITY?

TEN AND TEN.

HOW ABOUT SHANNON?

UM...I DON'T WANT TO GIVE NUMBERS.

SHANNON ALWAYS HAS THE BEST GAMES.

WALKING TO SCHOOL THE NEXT DAY...

HEY SHANNON.

UH, HI JENNY.

YOU ALWAYS MAKE UP THE BEST GAMES.

THANKS!

I'VE BEEN THINKING ABOUT A GAME WE COULD PLAY AT RECESS. IT'S CALLED SEWER. SO THE TETHERBALL POLE IS THE SEWER...

THAT MORNING AT RECESS...

...AND WHOEVER GETS THROWN IN THE SEWER HAS TO STAY TILL A FREE PERSON GETS PAST THE GUARDIANS--

DON'T YOU DARE TELL ON ME.

YOU'RE SUCH A BABY, SHANNON! YOU CAN STAY OUT HERE AND FREEZE!

WHAT ARE YOU DOING?

YOU'RE SUCH A BABY, CYNTHIA! JUST MIND YOUR OWN BUSINESS!

BEFORE, I'D ALWAYS BEEN SURE MOM WAS ON MY SIDE.

HOW'S SCHOOL?

FINE.

HOW ARE YOUR FRIENDS TREATING YOU?

FINE.

I WAS TOO BUSY TO TALK ANYWAY.

I HAD TO FLEX MY LEGS EACH TIME WE PASSED A TREE.

IF WE DIDN'T END ON AN EVEN NUMBER OF TREES, I FELT YUCKY. EMPTY.

...FIFTY-TWO, FIFTY-THREE...

WHENEVER IT WAS JUST ADRIENNE AND ME, I FELT BETTER.

...AND THEN MAYBE THE RUNAWAY ORPHANS GET CAUGHT--

THEY GET CAUGHT? OOOH!

YEAH, BUT THEY ESCAPE THROUGH A SECRET TUNNEL...

INTO A MYSTERIOUS BOAT.

PULLED BY MERMAIDS!

I WISHED ADRIENNE WOULD LEAVE THE GROUP WITH ME.

IT WAS ONE OF MY FAVORITE DAYDREAMS.

A REVOLUTION!

SOMETIMES I WISHED...

OH, THIS? THIS IS JUST MY PET LION SHASTA.

I TRIED TO TURN THIS DAYDREAM INTO A STORY...

READY

...BUT IT STAYED IN MY HEAD. I COULDN'T SEEM TO WRITE STORIES ALONE.

WHEN I FINALLY DID ASK ADRIENNE...

PLEASE QUIT THE GROUP WITH ME. WE DON'T NEED THEM. WE CAN FORM OUR OWN GROUP.

BUT THEN THEY'D BE MAD AT ME.

BESIDES, I LIKE HAVING MORE FRIENDS THAN JUST YOU.

I WANTED ALL THOSE FEELINGS TO STOP.

TAP
TAP
TAP

...SIXTY-TWO, SIXTY-THREE,

...SIXTY-FOUR, SIXTY-FIVE...

I IMAGINED DYING.

SOMETIMES I TRIED TO RUN AWAY.

BUT MY IMAGINATION GOT IN THE WAY.

MAYBE IF I TRIED HARD ENOUGH...

ZARA
&
VERONICA

FOR FIFTH GRADE, I'D PUT IN FOR MRS. BRENNAN BECAUSE MY OLDER SISTERS HAD BEEN IN HER CLASS.

I DIDN'T KNOW, BUT MOST OF THE GROUP HAD PUT IN FOR MRS. LAROCHELLE. EVEN ADRIENNE.

YOU'LL STILL BE ABLE TO PLAY WITH YOUR FRIENDS AT RECESS.

ADRIENNE'S IN MRS. LAROCHELLE'S. JEN'S IN MRS. LAROCHELLE'S.

DO YOU KNOW ANYONE IN YOUR CLASS?

JUST AMY AND NICOLE.

YOU COULD INVITE THEM TO CAMP...

TREFOIL RANCH, SUMMER 1984.

AMY HAD ALWAYS BEEN NEAR THE END OF JEN'S LINEUP.

NICOLE WAS A NEW MEMBER OF THE GROUP. SHE'D MOVED INTO OUR SCHOOL IN THE MIDDLE OF FOURTH GRADE.

MAYBE WITH TWO FRIENDS IN MY CLASS, FIFTH GRADE WOULD BE OKAY.

HEAVENLY FATHER, PLEASE MAKE THIS A GOOD YEAR. PLEASE LET THE GROUP BE NICE TO ME...

MY LAST DAY OF SUMMER TRADITION: READING IN MY BACKYARD.

I DIDN'T FIND OUT UNTIL LATER, BUT THE REST OF THE GROUP SPENT THE LAST DAY OF SUMMER PLAYING TOGETHER.

I MADE A FOOLPROOF PLAN FOR SUCCESS IN THE NEW SCHOOL YEAR.

FOURTH GRADE SHANNON

GLASSES

PATHETIC

FIFTH GRADE SHANNON

NO GLASSES!

CONFIDENT!

POPULAR!

Welcome to Mrs. Brennan's Fifth/Sixth Split

THAT'S WHY I DIDN'T KNOW MOST OF THE PEOPLE ON THE CLASS LIST...

I DID IT.

AT LAST.

VICTORY!

I WAS FINALLY FREE.

I WASN'T SURE LEAVING THE GROUP WAS THE RIGHT CHOICE.

AT LEAST I'D HAD FRIENDS.

BRIINNGGG

NOW SOMETIMES I WAS SO SAD I COULD BARELY BREATHE.

SO I TRIED ONE LAST TIME.

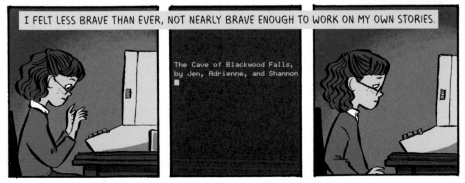

I FELT LESS BRAVE THAN EVER, NOT NEARLY BRAVE ENOUGH TO WORK ON MY OWN STORIES.

The Cave of Blackwood Falls, by Jen, Adrienne, and Shannon

BUT I COULD IMAGINE THEM.

144

RECESS WAS THE HARDEST.

HI SHANNON.

LACEY WAS A SIXTH GRADER IN ANOTHER CLASS. I KNEW HER FROM CHURCH.

HEY LACEY!

I WAS WONDERING IF I COULD MAYBE PLAY WITH YOU GUYS?

REBECCA DOESN'T WANT TO HANG OUT WITH A FIFTH GRADER. SORRY.

147

THE STOMACHACHES, THE WORRYING. AND SHE'S ALWAYS COUNTING THINGS.

SOUNDS LIKE ANXIETY. LOTS OF KIDS GROW OUT OF IT. SHANNON, TRY NOT TO WORRY SO MUCH.

OKAY.

IT WAS A LONG AUTUMN.

BUT WHEN WINTER CAME, SOMETHING CHANGED.

MRS. BRENNAN MADE US MOVE THE DESKS, AND I WAS SITTING BESIDE SOMEONE NEW.

HER NAME WAS ZARA, AND SHE WAS...

COOL.

WHO WAS THAT?

THE GROUP.

THEY WERE YOUR FRIENDS?

YEAH...

ZARA AND VERONICA JUST WALKED AROUND AND TALKED.

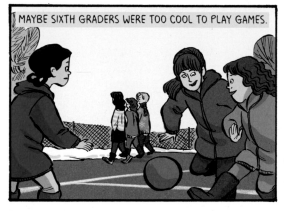

MAYBE SIXTH GRADERS WERE TOO COOL TO PLAY GAMES.

APPARENTLY, SIXTH GRADERS WERE ALSO TOO COOL TO WEAR PARKAS AND MOON BOOTS.

WHO NEEDS A PARKA? NOT ME!

I THANK THEE FOR NEW FRIENDS.

AND PLEASE PLEASE FORGIVE ME FOR CALLING THE GROUP MEAN NAMES. I PROMISE I WON'T CALL PEOPLE NAMES EVER AGAIN...

I LEARNED ABOUT VERONICA'S MOTHER'S NEW BOYFRIEND, AND ZARA'S BROTHER'S FLIRTY FRIENDS.

THEY WERE NICE TO EVERYONE.

HEY DAWN.

IT WAS A NEW KIND OF POPULAR.

HI BECCA.

THERE WAS A PLACE ON THE FIELD WHERE THE SNOW MELTED INTO A DITCH AND TURNED YELLOW.

THAT LOOKS LIKE A PEE HOLE.

WHAT?

THAT'S A LOT OF PEE. HOW MANY PEOPLE HAD TO PEE IN THERE TO FILL IT UP?

OR DID, LIKE, AN ELEPHANT PEE IN THERE?

UH-OH, DID I SAY SOMETHING STUPID?

YOU'RE FUNNY.

AND YOUR HAIR IS SO PRETTY. I ALWAYS WANTED RED HAIR.

GROWN-UPS SOMETIMES SAID RED HAIR WAS "CUTE," BUT KIDS ALWAYS THOUGHT IT WAS "WEIRD."

ARE YOU SERIOUS?

TOTALLY. RED HAIR IS EXOTIC.

RECESS. TOMORROW. MEET AT THE PEE HOLE.

THE NEXT DAY, I RISKED BEING BABYISH AND INTRODUCED A GAME.

...THE SECRET AGENTS OF POOPDOM ARE TRYING TO FIND THE LOCATION OF THE PEE HOLE...

WE MUST PROTECT IT AT ALL COSTS...

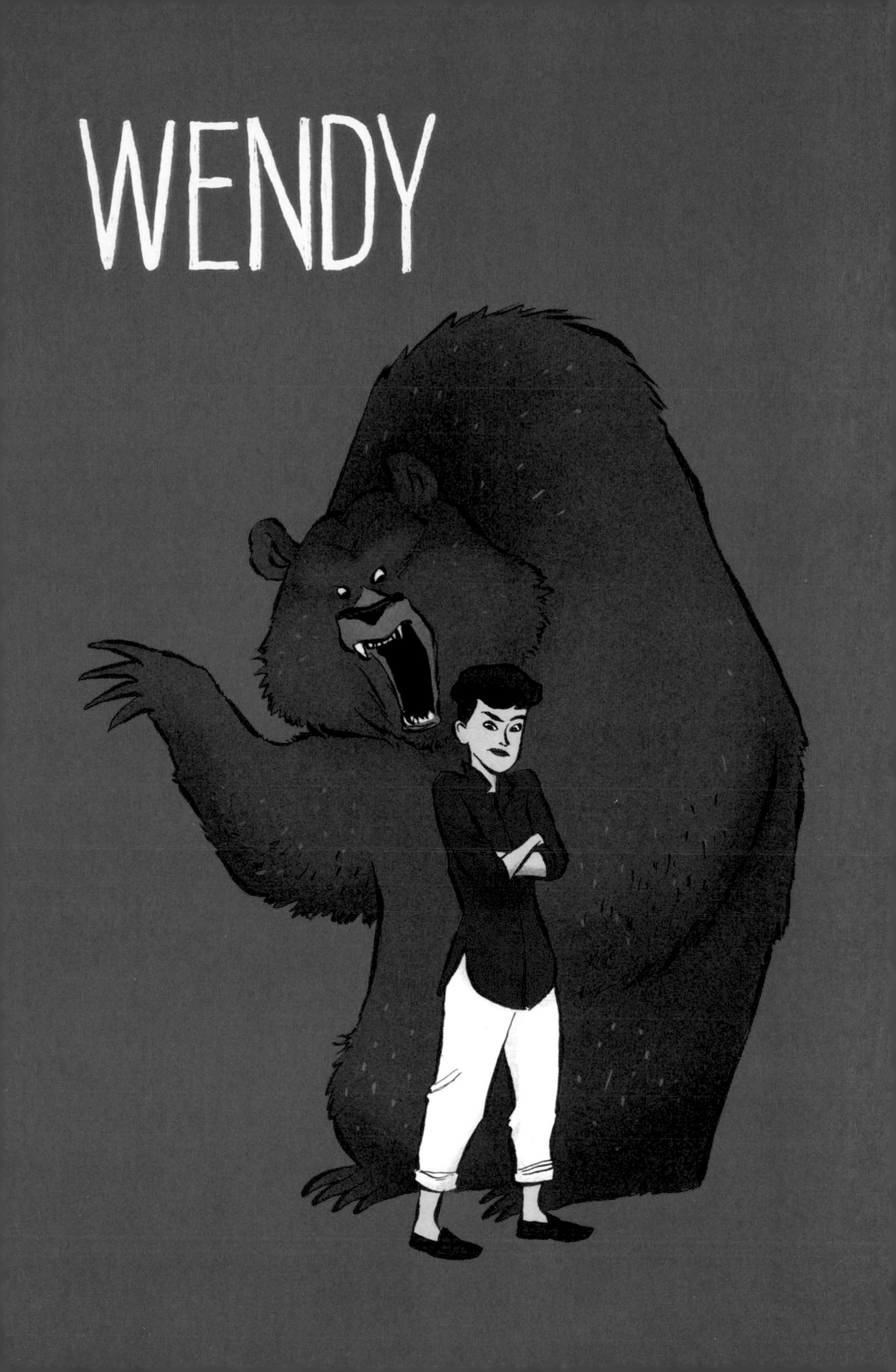
WENDY

MY FIRST MUSIC!

A WHILE LATER, WENDY PLANNED HER OWN PARTY.

I MEAN IT, I DON'T WANT SHANNON OR CYNTHIA OR JOSEPH COMING OUT AND RUINING IT--

OKAY, OKAY...

SHE'D INVITED A BUNCH OF PEOPLE TO COME OVER AFTER SOME HIGH SCHOOL GAME.

WHAT ELECTIVES DID YOU CHOOSE FOR NEXT YEAR?

I WAS WORRIED THAT JENNY WAS RIGHT. SUMMER WAS ONLY A WEEK AWAY.

UM, HOME EC...

HOME EC?

HECK YEAH, WE GET TO MAKE FOOD!

I DUBBSED TO SIT TO JEN'S RIGHT.

NO, I DID FIRST.

WELL I DUBS HER RIGHT TOMORROW.

I ALREADY DID.

FRIDAY THEN.

GUYS, CAN WE NOT ANYMORE WITH THIS?

BUT ALSO...WHAT? I'D IMAGINED JEN WAS LIKE THIS...

...BUT REALLY SHE WAS LIKE THIS?

REALLY? OKAY. I'D LIKE THAT.

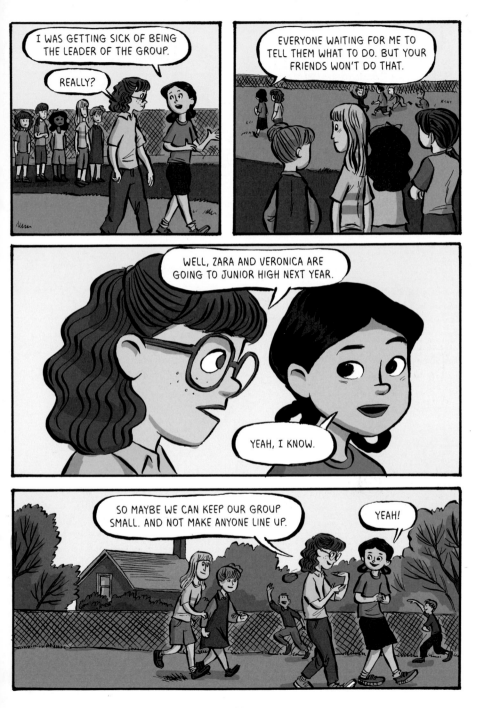

FOR FIELD DAY, OUR NEW GROUP WENT SHOPPING FOR OUTFITS IN THE LATEST STYLES.

FLUORESCENT COLORS

BIG BOWS

BIG LOOSE SHIRTS

MADONNA LACE GLOVES

MULTIPLE BELTS

WE JUST WALKED AROUND, PRACTICED BEING SIXTH GRADERS.

HI VICKI. HI MOLLY.

I WANTED TO TRY OUT ZARA AND VERONICA'S KIND OF POPULAR, THE NICE KIND.

HI REAGAN.

SOMETIMES I JUST WANNA GO

ARGH!!

ARGH!!

ARGH!!!!!

WRITE TO ME IN L.A. TELL ME WHAT HAPPENS WITH THE JENNIFERS.

OKAY.

PROMISE I'M THE FIRST PERSON YOU'LL TELL WHEN YOU HAVE YOUR FIRST KISS.

BLEH.

RIGHT AWAY I WROTE WENDY A LETTER.

ZZZZZZ-BEEP
ZZZZZZ-BEEP

Once upon a time there was a girl with red hair

who believed her destiny was to ride alone.

But an old evil was rising in the north lands.

. . . at the final moment, when all seemed to be lost,

she cried out for help.

The many friends she had made on her journey heard her call.

And they came running.

After all, no one's destiny is to be alone.

Author's Note

Some have said that memories are the stories we tell ourselves about our past. *Real Friends* is the story I've been telling myself about my elementary school years. If you were to ask the other people portrayed in this book how it happened, surely the story they've been telling themselves would be different from mine.

I never thought I would write a memoir. For one thing, I didn't have a tragic or extraordinary childhood. I had kind parents who loved me. I had friends and many good times. But I decided to write this book in order to share how those years felt to me, in case you have felt or are feeling the same way. And then we can say to each other, "Hey, me too! Isn't that something? To realize I'm not the only one?"

Most of the events in this book really happened. Or I think they did. I've learned that memories aren't 100 percent accurate, and there's so much I didn't record in my journals. But I did my best. The parts I couldn't remember exactly, I wrote as they might have happened (like the conversation where Zara and I first became friends). A few parts I changed on purpose to help the story flow (like moving up the year Wendy left home). And I renamed everyone except myself because my flawed memory can't perfectly portray real people.

If this were a fiction, I probably would have resolved the relationship with Jenny, but in real life, it was never resolved. Even though little Shannon really did say "no" when Jenny asked to join the "new group," it was still hard for me to write it. After all, I believe in forgiveness and redemption. But I chose to include it because I think it's okay to make boundaries between ourselves and anyone who has bullied us. It's okay to say no.

Though my friend troubles didn't all go away in sixth grade, as I kept growing up, it did keep getting better. In high school I got to know the girl who had been my hiding-behind-the-shrub companion. Her situation in elementary school had been so much harder than what I'd been facing. I wonder if I could have seen her loneliness more clearly if I hadn't been so wrapped up in my own, and if we could have been friends for each other.

I was sick a lot, and though my loving mom took me to many doctors, we never figured out what was wrong. The mysterious stomachaches and some of those sad, anxious, yucky feelings were probably symptoms of an anxiety disorder and mild obsessive-compulsive disorder. Today there are lots of resources for kids with mental health disorders. Cognitive behavioral therapy is an effective tool for anxiety and OCD, and starting therapy when young can help tremendously. The website adaa.org is a helpful resource.

The sister who inspired the character of Wendy also struggled with undiagnosed behavioral health disorders. Back then, no one really knew what to do for kids whose brains worked a little differently. As she grew up, she found her own group—friends who realized how funny, clever, vibrant, and fun she was. Maybe our reconciliation in real life didn't happen as quickly as it does in this book, but it felt that way. We corresponded regularly whenever she lived out of state. She was the first person I talked to about my first kisses, my boy troubles, and my writerly dreams. As adults we became great friends, and she became a devoted, loving, brilliant mother.

She is so much more than I've been able to show in this book. As are the rest of my family; the people I call Jen, Jenny, and Adrienne; and even little Shannon. We are, all of us, so much more than we are at our worst and at our best.

Friendship in younger years can be especially hard because our worlds are small. In high school and beyond, I found many supportive, lifelong friends. If you haven't found your "group" yet, hang in there. Your world will keep growing larger and wider. You deserve to have real friends, the kind who treat you well and get how amazing you are.

Kindergarten

Awww . . .

2ⁿᵈ Grade

Here I am, looking super hand-me-down-ish and forgotten-in-the-middle child.

3rd Grade

When I first joined The Group.

4th Grade

The year I decided to be a writer.

5th Grade

My retake photo—this time without glasses!

Acknowledgments

Special thanks from Shannon . . .

- to LeUyen Pham, who was exactly the right person to illustrate this book. This is as much your story as mine, Uyen. Thank you! Apologies to your family for all the long days and late nights you dedicated to this book. And cheers for Jane Poole and her magnificent help on the coloring.
- to Connie Hsu, my editor, who literally made this book possible. Thanks for taking my nonsense of a first draft and patiently talking me through twenty or so revisions until I got it right.
- to all the First Second and Macmillan folk who have taken such care of me and this book, including Gina Gagliano, Mark Siegel, Andrew Arnold, Danielle Ceccolini, Allison Verost, Erin Stein, Jon Yaged, Angus Killick, Jennifer Gonzalez, Simon Boughton, Lucy Del Priore, Katie Halata, Jill Freshney, Alexa Villanueva, and of course Connie Hsu, who I already mentioned but deserves being mentioned twice.
- to LeUyen Pham again, who is simply PHAM-TASTIC! (If that's not a thing yet, I'm going to make that a thing. You're welcome.)
- to Cece Bell, Jenni Holm, Emily Wing Smith, Aaron Hartzler, Raina Telgemeier, Coe Booth, and Sherri Smith, for the advice and inspiration.
- to the Bryner family, for the stories, the laughter, the forgiveness.
- to Ava Cabey and Avarose, Samantha Stewart, and Rebecca Jensen Maw, for friendship and insight.
- to Margaret Stohl and the YALLWEST crew, for huddling me in right when I needed it.
- and to Dean, Max, Maggie, Wren, and Dinah, who were the best beta readers in the history of the universe.

Special thanks from Uyen . . .

- to Shannon Hale. My head knows that you wrote this story. But my heart is still convinced that somehow you crawled inside my memories and handpicked all these events and feelings and insecurities from my childhood and called them your own. My husband likes to joke that if I had just swapped out the Salt Lake City neighborhoods for the Los Angeles suburbs, and your large Mormon family for my own large Vietnamese Catholic family, and lastly changed little Shannon's hair color from red to black, then this book is about me. Hopefully I've managed to crawl into your head and draw out your memories as well. You are forever a kindred spirit.
- to Connie Hsu, who went through every page, every panel, every face, and let me know when I got it just right. Like Ginger Rogers and Fred Astaire, we had to dance it just right, and you were the perfect dance partner. But which are you, Ginger or Fred?
- to Mark Siegel, for making me always believe I'm better than I am. It makes me never want to disappoint you.
- to the First Second and Macmillan crew, who I've worked with forever now it seems. How do you guys manage to do what you do with what little you have to do it with? I've never known a more devoted group than you. Special shout out to Andrew Arnold, who came out of nowhere and gave us that last push we needed over the finish line.
- to my colorists, Jane and Max, who pulled off the most amazing feat of labor since Hercules was challenged, and in far less time. I threw you into the deep end, and you're still talking to me. How is that possible? And I still owe you dinner . . .
- to Leo and Adrien, whose faces are still the faces of every character I draw. It is unbelievable how much I love you guys.
- to Alex. For absolutely everything.

Shannon Hale is the *New York Times*–bestselling author of many children's and young adult novels, including the popular Ever After High series and multiple award winners *The Goose Girl, Book of a Thousand Days,* and *Princess Academy,* a Newbery Honor book. She co-wrote the graphic novels *Rapunzel's Revenge* and *Calamity Jack* and the best-selling chapter book series The Princess in Black with her husband, Dean Hale. They live with their four children near Salt Lake City, Utah. **shannonhale.com**

LeUyen Pham is the *New York Times*–bestselling illustrator of The Princess in Black series with Shannon and Dean Hale and *Freckleface Strawberry* with Julianne Moore. She wrote and illustrated *Big Sister, Little Sister, The Bear Who Wasn't There,* and is the illustrator of numerous other picture books, including *The Boy Who Loved Math.* She lives and works in Los Angeles with her husband and her two adorable sons. **leuyenpham.com**